Advance
Everything is Ret...
Todo Vuelve a la Tierra

*Briana's **Everything is Returned to the Soil** lets the conviction of her dreams, fantasies, heartaches, darkness, prayers and experiences mirror the human side of all of us, her Poetry paints the ancestry and pain of society.*

— Juan Cardenas, Associate Director of Los Angeles Poet Society, Teacher with California Poets in the Schools, and author of *The Beat of an Immigrant Chicano*

*Briana Muñoz's book, **Everything is Returned to the Soil/ Todo Vuelve a la Tierra**, is a collection of poetry that documents heartache like only a well-tongued Poet can. The extremities of mind, body, and spirit, are all fed through the grinder, smoothed out, and laminated for us to see.*

You can feel it in Briana's poems, and recollections of love, that pierce like an unwanted thorn between the eyes. Her sensual language shows us how fierce the exchange of love can be and how the scars belong like bandages. If you exorcise away the torment of thoughts, songs, clothes, scents, and the hard-on memories of once love – this book will take place of the razor over your arm, and toast you with a double shot, and a finger to your ex-lover.

Jump into this book and empower yourself away from the drunk-dial, sloppy text, or lonesome one-nighters. Muñoz's book is medicine for the freshly wounded. It is also a beautiful homage to ancestry, madre tierra, and the freest feminine spirit!

Briana writes with such strength, and honors her lineage with her breath, blood, and ink. Poems like Elvira, which is an intimate vignette of grandmother to granddaughter exchanges, and an undertone of resentment for the impact of the patriarchy and colonization that white wash our families, painting over our cultura. Poems like, For my Mother, a life of the party woman, has such strong spirit, and Ancestral Wounds could be its own manifesto as she takes us on a journey to decolonize her past. Briana is unafraid to speak, unafraid to shed saliva, and unafraid to use her tongue.

— Jessica M. Wilson, MFA, Founder of Los Angeles Poet Society, Poet, Activist, Educator

Briana Muñoz's poetry wants to jump off the pages and dance. All sorts of dances — from traditional ceremonial Danza to dirty dancing. She has no problem juxtaposing sin with the sacred. And should she? Life is all of it. This book is a journey, a look into the depths of want with no disclaimers. Of people living ordinary lives and striving for the best lives they can get. We travel LA streets, visit its iconic neighborhoods and landmarks, go to the southern border with Mexico, even to La Habana. Throughout all of it, there is a profound reverence for ancestors and what they have to teach us as Indigenous peoples. At the same time, there's a fearless look at the complexities of women who are willing to be exactly who they choose to be. Cultural and societal shackles be damned. I was lucky to curate Briana's first book **Loose Lips** which I thought was bold, raw, and beautiful. **Everything is Returned to the Soil** is more of the same powerful poetry, only with more punch and more conviction. ¡Ajuua y Adelante!

— Odilia Galván Rodríguez, author of *The Color of Light: Poems for the Mexica and Orisha Energies*

Briana Muñoz's poetry confronts social injustices while proving that emotional vulnerability is a requisite for true strength, rather than a hinderance. There is a quiet tenderness in her words as she examines the everyday moment, or reflects on her identity, that contrasts with a building tension of inner conflict and acceptance that explodes on the page in a rush of beauty. This collection warrants multiple reads to experience the complexity that lies beneath the layers of meaning.

— Zachary Jensen, Poet, Writer, Translator, and Editor

poesia for the people!

—Briana

EVERYTHING IS RETURNED TO THE SOIL/ TODO VUELVE A LA TIERRA

FLOWERSONG
PRESS

A BILINGUAL POETRY COLLECTION
by Briana Muñoz

FLOWERSONG
PRESS

FlowerSong Press
Copyright © 2021 by Briana Muñoz
ISBN: 978-1-953447-85-2
Library of Congress Number: 2021939113

Published by FlowerSong Press
in the United States of America.
www.flowersongpress.com

Cover Art by Johnny Quintanilla
Cover Design by Priscilla Celina Suarez
Translations by Ana Maria Flores
Set in Adobe Garamond Pro

EVERYTHING IS RETURNED TO THE SOIL/ TODO VUELVE A LA TIERRA

A BILINGUAL POETRY COLLECTION
by Briana Muñoz

ACKNOWLEDGEMENTS

A kind thank you to the following literary journals for printing and sharing my poems:

"Raiz" has appeared in *La Bloga*, the *Poets Responding* page, and in the *Oakland Arts Review*.

"Gente" has appeared in the *Dryland* literary journal. A publication based in South-Central Los Angeles showcasing words by POC.

Gracias *Dryland*.

"Release It" has appeared in *Boundless: The Anthology of the Rio Grande Valley International Poetry Festival*.

Tlazocamati to all.

FROM THE AUTHOR

As I began identifying the themes in my poetry, I noticed one thing. I noticed that everything stems from Mother Earth and everything returns to her. Love. Spirituality. Medicine work. Politics. Cultura. Traditional practices. The delicious food prepared by my abuela. Existence.

2019 was my year of a spiritual awakening and personal growth. My year of returning to my roots and further connecting to my Mexica lineage.

Some poetry is surface level, observant of raza around me, while other poetry in this collection touches at the prickly pear heart inside my chest.

Poems as a call to who I am as a woman, as a daughter to an immigrant, and as a walker of the Earth. Poems of declaration. Poems asking for forgiveness. Poetry of healing. Poems written in realization of how the universe works for us so we should work for her.

Everything is returned to the soil. Todo vuelve a la tierra. Sacred soil. Thank you.

For my parents.
For my grandparents.
For the teachers.
For Mother Earth.
For the ancestors.

Para mis padres.
Para mis abuelos.
Para los maestros.
Por la madre tierra.
Para los antepasados.

TABLE OF CONTENTS

My Tongue is a Thunderbolt

My tongue is a thunderbolt
at the mic, but a soft song
strummed at a coffee shop,
otherwise.

It is passive (unless triggered).
It is pleasure against soft skin,
in dimly lit bedrooms.

My tongue is only truth
and never slurs or silenced.
My tongue is "trouble",
he tells me, with a side
shy smirk.

My tongue remembers conquest
and knows the language
sang by spirit and ancestors,
never taught in classrooms.

My tongue
speaks universal love
and only love.
My tongue is a tool
used with caution.

My tongue is power.
It is knowledge.

It is occasional sadness
(and whiskey-driven madness).

My tongue is torture to self
at 3 AM
but also the medicine of a mother
to men who have lost their way,

but know that
I didn't choose it that way.

My tongue invites
Tonantzin Coatlicue,
calls to Grandfather
Xiutekutli.

My tongue tastes sorrow
through every ex-lover
to hurt myself all over again.
(It makes for good poetry, I guess.)

My tongue knows no satisfaction
until every child is fed.
My tongue welcomes
soft men in paisley prints
and dissolves tabs of LSD.

My tongue
todavia te quiere.
Toxic man,
one true love.

My tongue is a thunderbolt
(in training).

My Poem Isn't a Persuasive Essay

How many more poems do we need to write
until the children are
hopscotch-ing,
feet against white-lined
shapes against asphalt,
rather than in cages?

How much longer
do we continue
psychotically scribbling:
"Smash the Patriarchy"
"No War with Iran"
"Water is Life"
"Black Lives Matter"
"Give the poor kid medical attention.
The cold floor is no place
for their last breath, Goddammit"?

How many more hands
angrily performing stanzas?
Lips releasing spit of rage
and helplessness.

Poets stand up
because we hardly know how else to help,
because if we don't vomit
out metaphors,
it might be my breakfast.

Poets stand up
in response to your lack of credibility,
toddler-President tweets.

My lord!
My poem isn't a persuasive essay
for your vote.
My poem is a cry for help

released by pen and page.
My poem is a shout.
It is an airstrike
on your country club.

How many more Langston Hughes'?
How many more grandmothers
holding signs that read
"I can't believe I'm still protesting this shit"?

How many more Maya Angelous?
How many more Allen Ginsbergs?
Howls of anti-war?
How many more John Lennons?
Bed-ins for peace?
How many more banned books?

Your White House is filled with
cis-gendered white men,
dominating Mother of Mary
in fishnets, underneath
her faintly blue mantle.

Donald Trump,
oh how I've grown sick of that name,
regulating uteruses,
teasing her clit with your AR- 15s,
blood on fingertips.

My poem isn't a persuasive essay
on gun control but
how many more children?
Answer me.
This isn't a rhetorical question.
How many more poets?
How many more martyrs?
How many more pipelines?
How many more oil spills?
How much more spilled blood?

How many more traumatic brain injuries
until your stomachs feel satisfied?
How many more doors do my
small knuckles
need to knock on?
Write a poem
describing your thoughts on war.

Mi Poema No Es un Ensayo Persuasivo

¿Cuántos poemas más necesitamos escribir
hasta que los niños
jueguen a la rayuela,
pies contra líneas blancas,
formas contra el asfalto,
en lugar de en jaulas?

¿Cuànto tiempo más
continuaremos
garabateando psicóticamente:
"Aplastar al Patriarcado"
"No a la Guerra con Irán"
"El Agua es Vida"
"Las Vidas Negras Importan"
"Presten atención médica al pobre niño.
El piso frìo no es lugar
para su último aliento, maldita sea"?

¿Cuàntas manos màs
recitando estrofas con enojo?
Labios soltando saliva de furor
e impotencia.

Los poetas se ponen de pie
porque casi no sabemos de què otra forma ayudar,
porque si no vomitamos
metáforas
sería mi desayuno.
Los poetas se ponen de pie
en respuesta a tu falta de credibilidad,
Tweets berrinchudos
de Presidente.

¡Oh Dios mío!
Mi poema no es un ensayo persuasivo
por tu voto.
Mi poema es un grito de ayuda

publicado por pluma y página.
Mi poema es un grito;
es un ataque aéreo
a tu club campestre.

¿Cuántos más Langston Hughes?
¿Cuàntas abuelas màs
sosteniendo carteles que leen
"No puedo creer que todavía estoy protestando por esta mierda"?

¿Cuántos más Maya Angelous?
¿Cuántos más Allen Ginsbergs?
Aullidos de anti guerra?
¿Cuántos más John Lennons?
Bed-ins para la paz?
¿Cuántos libros más prohibidos?

La Casa Blanca está llena de
hombres caucásicos y cisgéneros,
dominando a Madre de María
con mallas, bajo
su manto azul claro.

Donald Trump,
¡Oh, cómo me he cansado de ese nombre!
regulando los úteros,
excitando su clítoris con tus AR-15,
sangre en las puntas de los dedos.

Mi poema no es un ensayo persuasivo
para el control de armas; pero,
¿Cuántos niños más?
Respóndeme.
Esta no es una pregunta retórica.
¿Cuántos poetas más?
¿Cuántos mártires más?
¿Cuántas oleoductos más?
¿Cuántos derrames de petróleo más?
Cuánta más sangre derramada?

¿Cuántas lesiones cerebrales traumáticas más?
¿Hasta que tus estómagos se sientan satisfechos?
¿Cuántas puertas más
necesito llamar con mis
nudillos pequeños?
Escribe un poema
describiendo tus pensamientos sobre la guerra.

Raiz

You tell me that my scars are hideous.
I respond by saying "Hideous, tu madre."

You formally inform me,
in a Times New Roman letter,
that my school work is below average.
I ask you,
"And exactly what is your definition of average?".

You laugh at the music blaring out of my
'93 nearly broken down, pick-up truck,
rusty paint chipping away
like the old folks at the country club.

But my music,
my music es de mi papa.
This music represents
beautiful colored women
in beautifully colored dresses,
multicolored ribbons,
floral headpieces.

Canciones de el pais de mis abuelos
Mexico Lindo,
what my nana calls it.

So please, continue making fun
of her thick, Spanish accent
while you sit there
ordering wet burritos and carne asada fries
from the Mexican food restaurant,
down the street from
the multi-million dollar homes,
in Del Mar.

Because my culture is beautiful
and so is my abuelita

in her plaid mandil and sweaty forehead,
and those mariachi lyrics I yell out proudly.

Beautiful are my dark eyebrows
which you make fun of
but I know they were passed down from my hard-working mother.
My culture is beautiful and
I refuse to allow you to tell me otherwise.

Ancestral Wounds

I am an empath,
a small body housing
overwhelming amounts of energy,
escaped from other homes.

I am the grief my grandmother never released.
I am decades of women
gathered around kitchens,
burnt fingertips,
but a poor cook
out of rebellion.

I am my own hurt
clothed around my neck
like a feather boa,
snaked around ankles,
like serpentine shackles.

I am my father
and my mother
and their father
and their mother.

Scarred of slapped wrists
for speaking the Spanish language
in El Paso during the mid-'30s.

I am heavy,
weighed down by cries
of ancestors.

Somehow, I am
the colonized and the colonizer,
from birth.

I am a dance,
of praise

of thanks,
a dance for independence,
drumbeat of resilience.

I am a horse on hind legs.
I am a horsewhipped
and the nourishment the horse consumes.

I am an empath,
a small body housing
overwhelming amounts of energy
escaped from other homes.

Heridas Ancestrales

Soy empática,
un pequeño cuerpo resguardando
cantidades abrumadoras de energía,
escapadas de otros hogares.

Soy el dolor que mi abuela jamas soltó.
Soy décadas de mujeres
reunidas alrededor de la cocina,
yemas de los dedos quemados,
pero una pobre cocinera
por su rebeldía.

Soy mi propio dolor
ceñido alrededor de mi cuello
como una boa emplumada,
serpenteado alrededor de los tobillos,
como grilletes serpentinos.

Soy mi padre
y mi madre
y su padre
y su madre.

Cicatrizado de muñecas abofeteadas
por hablar el idioma español
en El Paso a mediados de los años 30.

Soy pesada,
abrumada por los lamentos
de antepasados.

De alguna manera, soy el
colonizado y el colonizador,
desde el nacer.

Soy una danza

de alabanza,
de agradecimiento,
una danza por la independencia,
golpe de tambor de resiliencia.

Soy un caballo elevado en sus patas traseras.
Soy un caballo azotado
y el alimento que consume el caballo.

Soy empática,
un pequeño cuerpo resguardando
cantidades abrumadoras de energía,
escapadas de otros hogares.

Gente

Bartender (who got her BA in Spanish Lit)
reading Lorca at an open mic,
with her hand in her back pocket,

Whittier street juggler,
with a bow tie and striped socks

"I thought they only do this at La Linea
as folks wait to cross back."

Old man feeding LA street pigeons
at a bus stop
like it's his day job,

Mariachi woman
at Mariachi Plaza,

"You belong there, just as much as they do."

Man who asked me for change on my way to work,
man who asked me for change on my way back from work,
man who asked me for change in the parking lot,
woman with knotted hair
who was yelling
in front of Burrito King,
in Echo Park on a Saturday night

"I wish I had more to give."

Child who hustles chocolate bars
to support his basketball team, field trip,

Artist selling his mixtape
in Venice Beach,
like it's still 1998,

Paletero man,

tamale woman
pupusa-selling-grandmother
at the mat

"It is tempting, pero soy vegetariana."

Aztec dancers
at Ruben Salazar Park
with chachayotes wrapped around ankles
which resemble
tree leaves shaking

"Your dancing is healing our universe."

Punk kids
hipster kids
psychedelic, Spanish music-making kids

"Keep expressing yourselves."

Release It

I want to live in the bedroom tunes played
for me on your guitar.
I want to live in our highs and cancel our lows.
I want to discard all of the words you calculate
carefully to execute the lowest blow.
I want to live in your hands pinning mine down.
I want to exist in the journal I gifted you
but have never been let into.
I want to drown out the sound of you slut-shaming me.
I want to erase all former lovers,
letter by letter, until it's only your name on the chalkboard.
I want to hold the feeling,
cradle it,
release it,
and know we made the right decision.
I want to be reassured by you,
not always but every so often.
I want to scribble it on the walls.
I want to shout it.
I want to live in those first few months.
I want to position it,
wedged between sunset and sundown.
I want to be the hair tucked behind each other's ears.
I want the manic,
the empathetic,
the "I'm driving you to drink" statements.
I want you to believe that
I am sick-to-my-stomach sorry.
I want to erase every ounce of resentment.
I want to be the first person you think to call
when you need to be talked down from jumping.
I want you
more than I've ever longed for anything.
I want to stop pretending that I'm ok
and actually feel ok
`and I want to release the breath I've been holding.

July in Havana

Water drips outside of our casita,
claps,
like the hands de las mujeres morenas
as they dance to a Cuban folk song.
Bailando bailando,
the rhythm rocks me to sleep.

Julio en La Habana

Agua gotea afuera de nuestra casita
aplaude,
como las manos de las mujeres morenas
mientras bailan
con la canciòn folclórica Cubana.
Bailando bailando,
el ritmo me arrulla a dormir.

For JPH

Somewhere along the American Spirit tobacco
your fingers rolled into sloppy cigarettes and
the LSD fed to us by strangers in the desert, I
came to know you.
Removed the layers-
the sunglasses you wore to hide with your anxiety
the "Home" t-shirt,
the laces of your leather shoes,
and all defense mechanisms that attacked like a
cat pounce after you'd become 6-drink-deep-defensive.
I knew the real JPH.
You told me about your mother's hair salon
and how it was placed on Coast Highway in
between Juanita's Mexican Food and the
record store. You recounted the more-difficult.
The I've-never-told-anyone-this-before. You
 told me about the going away to get better.

In the mornings, you'd jitter your way toward
the inch of what was left in the old whiskey
bottle and come back to bed. Laughing you'd
say, "It's five o'clock somewhere", only
slightly ashamed.

Sin and Tonic

I am sorry for all the drinks
I poured, generously
and the men
who helped themselves.

I am sorry
for every sloppy word
I've ever spoken
at 2 in the morning
while you sat at home.

I am sorry that
you only meant more to me,
than that second drink,
on the weekdays

and your ultimatums
didn't quite
shake or stir me, enough

and only until when morning came
I'd acknowledge your points,
in the argument.
I am sorry.

Soft Girl

I am kind because
my Mother taught me to be.
I am a lover because
the planets demand that of me.

I have hurt myself
over and over and over again
in the process of
attempting to heal others.

At night, I retreat
and I kiss my own wounds.

I would rather leave here
exhausted and bruised
than to know that
there was more love I could've
whispered into the world.

Elvira

Grandma tells me about the slaughtering
of her name
in primary school.
How 6 letters converted to 4,
V-E-R-A.
Elvira means truth.

Grandma tells me about handsome men
in zoot suit, slick back, polished shoes.
(She tells me with a smirk.)

Grandma is a Taurus.
A bull, but sentimental.

She cries to Sarah McLaughlin,
shelter dog commercials
among other things,
like the graduation song
and church boys singing
"Ave Maria".

Grandma tells me
to find a boyfriend
but not to marry
and makes sure to ask me
for updates, every single time I visit.

Grandma tells me about
Grandpa's infidelity.
Tells me to lock my windows,
to watch out for the viejos
(and the hippies).

Grandma tells me her frijoles de la olla secrets.
She says she always keeps a pot of them
in the fridge.

Offers me fresh-squeezed lemonade
or jugo de naranja
which her small hands craft.

My grandma tells me a lot of things.
A storyteller, like myself.
She tells me about losing her son
and I can hear her cries
in the light, feet against wood,
creaking of her voice.

I'm a poet

"I'm a poet"
I shout.
And yes,
you are better off calling me-

Scum
Fuck
Poor
or Bum.

Sunday Dinner

Most days, my head
is too loud
like the clinking of forks
at our Sunday dinner

and the utensils
are spooned, stiffly, into my mouth
with reminders
of all of my
wrong movements
and all past mistakes.

Under Your Thumb

I started writing a poem
about your hands
today, again.

I made them
slide and slither
onto surfaces.

I made them penetrate
my body parts.

I wrote them into haikus,
too short.

I wrote them into
rhyme.

I kissed your palms.
Danced my tongue
around your pointer finger.

I made them speak.
I made them love me
like they used to

and scratch my head
to sleep.

I made them snap.
I made them clap.
I made them play a guitar tune.

I smudged tears from cheeks
with fingertips
and lifted coffee cups up
to touch your bottom lip.

I started writing
your hands into poetry again
but decided
that I was tired
of the grasp, around my pen.

You cannot do the healing for others

When you are ready
to shed your hurt
I will be here
standing with a set of arms reached out
welcoming you home.

For my Mother, a life of the party woman

I am a wild woman,
greñuda woman,
shut your lips type of woman,
dance on tabletops kind of woman.
I am made from my grandmother's stubborn rib
and my great grandmother's had-too-much-to-drink liver,
made from the dirt on the faces of children at play,
and from the sweat of my father
working underneath a summer sun.
I am a wild woman,
uncensored kind of woman,
a "You don't like me? You can leave" sort of woman,
don't need your permission kind of woman,
as a matter of fact, I make the rules type woman.
I am a warrior doll woman
but a treat others with kindness woman.
I am a "Loose Lipped" woman,
word vomit woman,
Hair flying Wild With The Wind woman,
scares the men away woman,
made from the hands that patty-cake masa into tamales
made from hooves of horses
and my mother's soles dancing, tap tap, for the universe.
I am
a wild woman.

March 16, 2020
In a friend's art studio during the
Corona Virus quarantine, in Los Angeles

Power to the poets.
Power to the punks.
Power to the women breastfeeding
on public benches.

Long live the accordion
at the backyard gig
and the organ pedals
and the womb that
created small fingers.

Power to the kids marching
for something they only
slightly believe in
(because at least they're not
sitting with their silence).

Bless the alcoholics
in recovery
and the bum
asking for change on
the Venice Beach Boardwalk
(because at least he's being honest).

Bless the nun.
Bless the escort.
Bless the junkie.

Bless the priest who
doesn't molest small children
(or maybe fuck him too
by association).

Glory be to the

saggy breasts of my grandmother
and to the uncircumcised penis
and the teeth that accidentally graze it.

Praise the pen who tells the truth.
Praise the pen that rhymes
and the keys slammed
in a depressive episode.
Hail the unpublished poet
who burns his prose.
(Fuck the pretentious.)

Praise the woman.
Praise the denimed dyke.
Praise the lipstick of the femme
and the non-binary
and the transgengered.

Power to the paint
and the brush
and the blank canvass.
Power to your inner monologue
as it is poetry, in itself.

Power to this page
and the weeping
that showers it.
Holy the Planned Parenthood clinic
and the pro-choice assistants
who escort young women in.

Sacred the prayers
sang by ancestors
and the incense being burned
in honor of them.
Power to the shaman
and the elders and the
unspoken wisdom of the fuego.

Power to the scoundrel
and the whiskey
that they bathe in.
Holy holy holy
the peyote and the mushroom
and the psychadelic sapo and the kambo.

Power to the teacher
who works a second job.
Sweet sacred
the cuffed pant-legged hipster
and the music.
Power to the children
who grow into their
curiosity versus against it.
Power to the parent
who is present.

Power to the spiral staircase
of the artist
Power to the people.

Famous Poets in the Sack

I imagine group sex with
Whitman and Poe.
Yes,
double poet penetration.

Being soft with Woolf,
tucking the hair behind her ear,
a soft grace
of lips
against her neck.

I imagine T.S. Eliot is
real vanilla.

Faking an "O"
with Hemingway.

That's usually how it goes
with those
Hills like White Elephants
toxic masculinity types.

Right?

BDSM with Plath.
Real passionate
baby-making with Neruda.
(Cries when he climaxes.)

Some trippy,
lava lamp lit, LSD
bedroom times with Ginsberg.

James Joyce spitting in my mouth.
I imagine
going down on Dickinson
and I get aroused.

How many poems (Part 2)

How many poems can I write
about my sadness
until they become a suicide letter?

How many more lines
stringed together
about your hands,

about the fine hair
caught between my teeth,
and the panting penetrating

my eardrum?
How many poems can I write
about your manipulative tongue

until I become those words,
until there are no more trees
to turn to paper?

Until there is no sun
or water
or soil.

How many poems can I burn
over stovetops?
How many poems can I puke out

to audiences of people
I do not know,
who will return to their homes,

and I
to my despair?
How many poems can I write?

Baby's Breath

I am almost certain,
as certain as you can be
about these type of things,

that I loved you
in a past life.

That I felt
the warmth of your fingertips
scratch against my back
to wake me up, in the mornings
on our lazy Sundays.

That we wed
against a backdrop,
bunches of baby's breath,
and guests clinked glasses
into the night,

and the bottoms of lace dresses
collected dust
from the dance floor,

that you were sober
and things were much easier
for us, in that lifetime.

That we had a home
and a dog
and a couple of naked babies,
running around our legs,
as we'd cook breakfast
and that there were a lot of laughs

and when there was sadness
(because there always is)
you would hold me

or I would fix up a hot bath for you
to soak in.

That you were consistent,
that you were present,
that the idea of us
wasn't toxic or far-fetched.

Dozens of synchronicities later
and I know this must be true,

that I knew you before I met you
at the local, stinks-of-urine and
bottom-shelved-booze,
sticky-counter-top bar,
the night I took you home.

And in that life
you didn't lose your mind
trying to minimize the pain
with the poppy.

And in that life
I didn't send sporadic
"Thinking of you" texts
just to make sure you hadn't died yet.

We are connected
further than time
and physical form,
beneath the spirals of your
callused hands and
roadways of your palms.

Two mystics
that found their way
back home.

I know this,

when you visit me in my dreams
and I know it was intentional,

When you drove two hours to visit
after you had heard "Harvest Moon"
only because it reminded you of me,

and later that day, at the restaurant,
it played
and I asked you if you could hear it.
I am no longer surprised
by these coincidences.

Resentment

Some days I feel as though
I could love you until I die;
other days,
my chest crawls with rage
and I remember that it is you
who has lit the match.

Resentimiento

Algunos días siento como si
podría amarte hasta que muera;
y otros dìas,
mi pecho se arrastra de ira
y recuerdo que eres tú
quien ha encendido el fósforo.

Bar in Boyle Heights

In a loud bar
on First Street,
you stand directly across from me
with your eyes fixed
following each movement
of mine, curiously.

I pucker my lips
toward my straw
while you watch me
like an art piece
nailed against a white wall
at a gallery,

and you,
maybe an art collector
studying me,
asking yourself
what the artist's intent was,
behind each stroke, silently
but regardless of that
you enjoy it.

I smile
and ask you what it is
that you want to tell me.
You say "Nothing",
smile back too.

The couple sitting in the
bar stools next to ours
may have been together a while.
Things seem comfortable.

I imagine that the woman
hovers over his shoulder
when he texts about boys night,

or that the man comments
on the length of her dress
when she gets ready in the mornings.

You try my drink
and I try yours,
lick the sugar off my lips
and anxiously,
you tell me,
that you really feel like painting.

Midnight Moon

In the hour of the moon
I await you
like a hungry cat
salivating,
pacing from end to end
eager to consume you.

Luna de Media Noche

En la hora de la luna
te aguardo
como una gata hambrienta
salivando,
yendo y viniendo de un lado a otro
ansiosa por consumirte.

MAKE LOVE TO THE POET

We speak about "The Hollow Men"
and we speak about Kipling.
You lick your fingertips
to turn pages,

move them gently, across my breasts
in the morning.

Your fingers become honey-pot drippy wet
from curiosity
in investigating my anatomy.

My mouth recites lines.
It moans.
It whimpers "Give me more",

sips coffee,
nervously drags a cigarette
while half of my body is
cozied up underneath your coat.

We speak about Hemingway
and you tell me
all of the things you want to do to me
once we get back home.

Kitchen Towels

I mean it when I tell you
that I want you
in every way,

our arguing about the color of kitchen towels,
my body bent over in bedrooms and my catching my breath
against night-sky walls,
your gathering my pieces off the concrete floor,
my sobbing,
your whispering that you've never seen
a more beautiful thing,

the just-because flowers you gift me,
the funeral home flowers
of your distant relative, I only met briefly,
two Christmases ago,

your threatening to leave me the next time
I'd have too much to drink,
your- not leaving me,
our "come back home"s,
your hands,
my hands,
my hands in your hands,
my fingers pulling at my own hair, fed up,
your driving to my workplace to apologize profusely,

your Sunday morning vinyl dance moves,
my on-all-fours
praising every god damned crease of your skin,
and every stupid freckle.

I mean it when I say
that I want you in every way.
I mean it when I say these things.

Home

And no matter how many bodies have housed
mine,
I have still, never felt so at home, as I do,
when I am behind closed doors, underneath
you.

Resilient Girl

Resilient girl,
I want to tell you
that it is O.K.

- to be still
- to tie your arms behind your back
and just, allow.

I want to tell you
that you are a whole universe
inside a small body.

You are capable.
You are deserving.

Resilient girl,
I want to show you
that winds aren't always wild,
that skies aren't always
clouded by manipulative words.

I wish for you to see
that it is O.K. to just,
be.

Tonantzin

Feel the earth.
Take your hands to her chest.
Dig your fingertips
under soil, slightly

just enough to
connect.

Abre tu Corazón
under Tonaltzintli.
Let them guide you.

Feel the rain.
Anoint your skin.
In doing this,
you will understand,
you are never alone.

Evening drive through DTLA

At golden hour
anything is beautiful,
even Downtown
even Skid Row.
The way the sun sits
so low,
hugging its children
shining humbly
but tired.

Monarch

My heart palpitates
Mexica
       monarch
            huēhuētl
warrior

but my primos
me dicen
"Pocha".

When the
mezcal
       guzano
            habanero
slide down my throat
with ease,

this is proof to them,
that my skin is not just this color
from a weekend
at Papas & Beer.

Hair braided
by hands of women
working
from sun-up
       to sun-down
and glitter, plastic beads.

Manitas reach out
toward me on the boardwalk
with hand-painted turtle
figurines.

I give the chiquilla
5 dollars

even though I am not in the market
for more nic nacs.

At the backyard party
my tongue trips over
itself
when I ask for "no meat".

The señoras roll eyes
and the men
wearing too much cologne
pat me down, like TSA,
but with their eyes.

I want to tell them that I
listen to Bowie
and they listen to Chalino;
therefore, it would just
never work out.

But when the Vicente Fernandez
comes into queue
I become my father.

One belch of
"Y volver, volver"
and suddenly I've got a
tortilla
        con carnitas
                y cervaza
on a summer day
panza,

sweat and dirt and leather horse reins,
a true vaquero.

Mother Earth speaks to me
in Nahuatl,

in Spanish,
and in my gringo English.

Calls me "Mija"
when I get frustrated,
like my tías,
but with less hairspray.

I left my heart on this Vegas hotel room pen pad

I left my heart with you
in your hands,
the same hands that wrap around my neck at night,
in twinkle-light bedrooms.

I left my heart in our Albany cottage bubble-bath bathtub,
in our Joshua Tree sunsets.
I left my heart in the windy roads of Topanga Canyon.

I left my heart in your 5 AM eyes,
in the inhaling and exhaling
of my head on your chest.

I buried it in the soil.
I buried it under the Salton Sea.

I left it in the old man asking us about our favorite literature.
I buried them,
stanza by stanza,
the poems you'd read to me
while your fingers, combing my hair,
sang me to sleep.

I left my heart in my pen and paper poems
written about you
and I swear I nearly quit poetry.

I left my heart with you,
in your hands.

After The Fact

Some days,
I close my eyes and whisper
all of the things I should've said to you but didn't,
trusting the universe to relay my message.

Dear (<u>Name of my Suicidal Friend</u>)

Often, I think of you
throughout my days and
before I go to bed.

I close my eyes
and speak to you.
I tell you that you are loved,
that you are well,
that you are whole.

I fill you with love
and light
and surround you, in it
likewise.

Often, I think of you
and I try to make you change your mind
about yourself.

I want to tell myself

I want to tell
the pitter-patter in my chest
to quiet.
That it is time for sleep.

That my mind is stronger
than the anxiety it
cohabits with.
I want to tell my lungs

to inhale only
self-respect
and exhale every ounce
of self-doubt.

Taking a 9-minute knee at the Los Angeles uprising for George Floyd

Protestors gather
Black folk
Brown folk
White folk
Filipinx folk
"Asians for Black Lives Matter"
You see them all.

Children
Middle-aged white men
the fire in the chests
of the millennials
Man walking with a limp
maybe from a bad knee
or perhaps old age

We chant
and cry
and dance
and beg
"Stop killing us".

At 3rd Street,
we block the intersection.
Cars honk
in support of what we are
saying here, today.

"Stop killing us."
Stop drawing your guns
on unarmed black youth.
Stop escalating matters.
Stop only holding officers accountable
when video footage goes viral.
We need change
but we need it year-round.

We halt to a stop
and energy buzzes
like auric vibrations.
We are one.
I feel my neighbor's pain
and they feel their neighbor's pain.

Organizers ask that we take a knee.
Skin against concrete,
feet blistered
and crying,
unto Tonanztin.

Our government might not hear us
or value bodies over profit
but she does.
Yes, she does.

An Apology is Not an Admission of Guilt

I have held plenty of hands
and spent enough time
wandering about,

like a man, barefoot
in ragged clothes,
in search of his next drink
or meal or cigarette.

I have slept aside warmth
to know it wasn't your warmth,
to know I would've rather slept alone.

I have counted down my days
until my end of day,

like an unhappy worker
tending the machines
at the old mill
eager for his shift to end.

I have stared at my hands so long
counting the wrinkles
and crevices,

line after line,
mimicking those of
Ginsberg's "Howl"
For Carl Solomon.

Hands that desire only your hands,
a mind that desires only your time.
I have done enough of these things
to know that

you will always be the answer

to every question
I will ask
in this lifetime.

Coffee Grinds

I watch you in the mornings
pouring water over your coffee grinds
and I know there are worries buzzing
in your mind.

I want to tell you
that it is O.K. to seek solace in me,

even when my energy is exhausted
I will gladly
give my remaining
to you.

Café Molido

Te observo en
las mañanas
vertiendo agua sobre tu café molido
y sé que hay preocupaciones zumbando
en tu mente.

Quiero decirte
que está bien buscar
consuelo en mí,

aùn cuando mi energía se encuentra exhausta
con gusto
daré mi restante
a tì.

Man who only reads 19th-century poets

"Come back home", I say,
as if your books still sit
interbred on my bookshelves,
classics with contemporary,
and you remind me
from the other room
to not set my coffee cups on them.

"Come back home"
like other hands haven't slid
against the slopes of my hips
and mouths haven't graced my breasts
since yours.

Like you never said that
I was just "another bitch".
How that slipped from your teeth,
your teeth
that would've ravaged through me
if your subconscious could speak.

I know
your resentment clinks louder now
than the love you feel for me.
I know that
you would rather forget
than repair
and I know that you can't seem to
get yourself to do that, either.

"Come back home", I say.
Creator knows
how many times I've whispered,
"Come back home".

Dancing Woman

It only makes sense
that I am this way
because of how my parents met.

The built-in nails underneath
the heeled dance shoes
worn against my mother's
skinny feet.

Tapped
into rhythm,
sweat
into rhyme.

Horse reins
and lassos
callusing my father's fingertips,

that grasped my mother's
as she slowed her breath
and imagined who I would look like most.

Bailarina

Solo tiene sentido
que soy como soy
por cómo se conocieron mis padres.

Los clavos incorporados debajo
de los zapatos de baile de tacón
calzados contra los pies delgados
de mi madre.

Zapateando
en ritmo,
sudor
en rima.

Riendas de caballo
y lazos
encallando las puntas de los dedos de mi padre,

que apresaron las de mi madre
mientras ella frenaba su aliento
e imaginò a cuàl de los dos me parecería más.

This Body

This body, my body,
that moves in routine
every day for me,
that rarely complains
how I praise you.

Heartbeat
like the huēhuētl of
the Indigenous peoples,
held with one hand
banged on by the other.

Toes that feel the earth
and vibrate with her
and like an empath,
they cry, releasing her sorrow.

Skin that changes
with the seasons
and through every
orbit around the sun,
how I praise you.

This body
who acts as home
for others
and with gratitude
they tend to every inch of it.

Lips to lobe,
lips to inner thigh,
lips to the freckle
of my left breast,
how they praise you, too.

"La Basilica / Body of the Femme"

Holy is the skin of a woman's breast.
Holy is the crease where leg meets hip.
Holy are her hands that dance as she speaks
and grasps and tie and create.
Holy are her truth-telling lips,
(unapologetic, powerful mujer).

"La Basílica / Cuerpo de la Dama"

Bendita es la piel del seno de una mujer.
Bendito el pliegue donde la pierna encuentra la cadera.
Benditas sus manos que danzan mientras habla
y atrapan y amarran y crean.
Benditos sus labios que dicen la verdad,
(sin disculpas, mujer poderosa).

Maria Del Rosario

My grandmother's hands
brew a pot of te de manzanilla,
hold infants,

always a hand
behind their heads
and noises released by lips to lull,

massage wounds
"Sana sana, colita de rana"
do not know the word "leisure".

My grandmother's hands
are blistered from burns,
comal: the culprit.

know how to hush,
know how to rock,
won't hesitate to pau pau.

crack walnut shells
with hand-held pliers,
sew all of the prom dresses
for all of the primas,

tie aprons
behind backs,

braid thick,
brown, long hair
hand over other hand
over hand.

My grandmother's hands
have buried her own mother
after years of putting out

cigarettes for her
and pouring out liquor.

I Want Peace

I want to
experience you,
from head to toe
from knee to crevice
freckle to scar
eyelash to navel

acting as if,
no time
has passed us
and no hurt
sits on our chests.

You,
my stubborn man
with all of your eccentricities
and your jabs
that remind me
that we are better off this way,

I will never stop
searching for you
in my happiest of places,
even when the feathers
of my wings
have all been plucked away.

Me,
your silent woman
who struggles to communicate
unhappiness
to keep you happy,
to eliminate gusts of wind
I stand battered,
by rain and thunder and
drenched feet.

I feel you, always,
under my brown skin
within the beating
of my Nahuatl heart,
at midnight,
under Venus,

and I tell you
que no quiero sentirte
just for one night.
I want slumber
and peace
and a chance to love
someone who is deserving.

Tongue Your Truths

It is not enough
to just speak your truths,
you must shout them.

You must sing them
into sky and storm
and sew them into soil,
to create

showers of lightning bolts
that electrocute
epiphany into the chests
of those around you.

Speak them
in a way that
others begin to memorize them,

in a way that others compare
your truths to
their truths.

Spit out hesitation
and doubt
like a wet loogie.

You must analyze them
under microscope.

Analyze them
from the four directions
and beyond,

Tlahuiztlampa,
Huiztlampa,
Cihuatlampa,

Mictlampa.

Purge them
from soul
and body
and mind.

Your truths should be told
in languages,
understood by all,
tongued into dialect,
danced into visual art.

Your truths should be exhausted,
wrestled every day,
held in a chokehold,
dehydrated.

Performed like
pageant queens
or show ponies,
filing claims to HR
for exploitation.

Ridden, like burros
at border towns,
realized during hot baths
or meditation.

Your truths should be sharp
like the edges of fenced wire
that skating scoundrels
hop over,
in attempts to outrun the cops.

Your truths
should never be muffled,
should never be held

under tongue
to keep the boat from rocking.

Your truths should
wreak havoc, against the
narrow-minded and obsolete.

Should know
no color
or sex
or class
or age.

Your truths should be jarred
and opened
on your difficult days
like ladybugs.

Penned aggressively,
carved into bathroom stalls
or tree bark.

Swallowed,
swished from right cheek
to left cheek
like red wine.

Your truths should never sell out.
Your truths should be rooted
beneath flesh
under rib

but they should grow
and extend
like the breath
of abuelita's pomegranate tree,

and the receding

and crashing
of the
salt-water sea.

Your truths should
exist
resist
and long live.

Transition

As I drove over the bridge on 1st Street,
white pillars that connect
mariachis to tent dwellers,
the golden hour illuminated
each direction of the panorama
and I thought about how
this must be, what it'll be like,
when Creator calls me home.

ABOUT THE AUTHOR

Briana Muñoz is a writer from Southern California. Raised in San Diego, she spent a lot of her time at her mother's Mexican folklore dance classes and at ranches where her father trained horses into the sunset. She is the author of *Loose Lips*, a poetry collection published by Prickly Pear Publishing (2019). Her work has been published in the Bravura Literary Journal, LA BLOGA, the oldest Chicana Chicano Literature blog in history, the Poets Responding page, and in the Oakland Arts Review, among others. In the 2016 publication of the *Bravura*, she was awarded the second-place fiction prize. Her poem "Rebirth" was featured in the Reproductive Health edition of the St. Sucia zine. Briana's work was one of ten chosen for The Best of LA BLOGA from 2015. When she isn't typing away, she enjoys Danza Azteca, live music, cats, and thrift shopping.